STEGOSAURUS

BY REBECCA SABELKO

EPIC

BELLWETHER MEDIA • MINNEAPOLIS, MN

EPIC BOOKS are no ordinary books. They burst with intense action, high-speed heroics, and shadows of the unknown. Are you ready for an Epic adventure?

This edition first published in 2020 by Bellwether Media, Inc.

No part of this publication may be reproduced in whole or in part without written permission of the publisher. For information regarding permission, write to Bellwether Media, Inc., Attention: Permissions Department, 6012 Blue Circle Drive, Minnetonka, MN 55343.

Library of Congress Cataloging-in-Publication Data

Names: Sabelko, Rebecca, author.
Title: Stegosaurus / by Rebecca Sabelko.
Description: Minneapolis, MN : Bellwether Media, Inc., [2020] | Series: Epic: The World of Dinosaurs |
   Includes bibliographical references and index. | Audience: Ages 7-12. | Audience: Grades 2 to 7. |
Identifiers: LCCN 2019003728 (print) | LCCN 2019010543 (ebook) |
   ISBN 9781618916600 (ebook) | ISBN 9781644870884 (hardcover : alk. paper) |
   ISBN 9781618917294 (paperback : alk. paper)
Subjects: LCSH: Stegosaurus--Juvenile literature.
Classification: LCC QE862.O65 (ebook) | LCC QE862.O65 S24 2020 (print) | DDC 567.915/3--dc23
LC record available at https://lccn.loc.gov/2019003728

Editor: Betsy Rathburn   Designer: Jeffrey Kollock

Printed in the United States of America, North Mankato, MN

TABLE OF CONTENTS

THE WORLD OF THE STEGOSAURUS

The stegosaurus was a huge dinosaur.
It is famous for the plates along its back and tail!
It walked the earth around 150 million years ago.
This was during the Late **Jurassic period.**

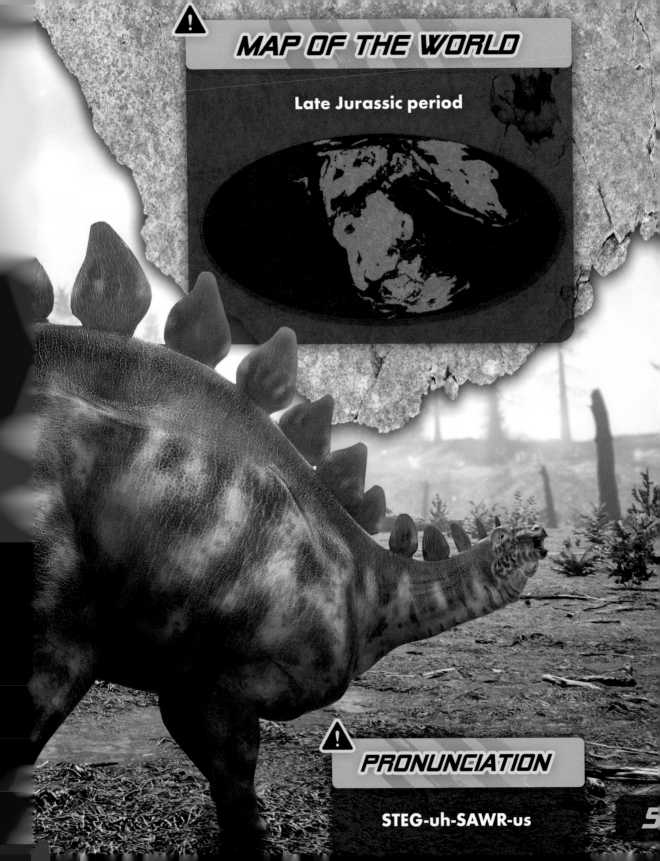

MAP OF THE WORLD

Late Jurassic period

PRONUNCIATION

STEG-uh-SAWR-us

WHAT WAS THE STEGOSAURUS?

The stegosaurus's plates were made of bone. But they were covered in skin!

Some people believe the plates took in heat from the sun. Others think the plates were used to show off to **mates**.

⚠ NAME GAME

The word *stegosaurus* means "roof reptile" in Latin.

The stegosaurus weighed around 4,000 pounds (1,814 kilograms)! Short front legs and long back legs made it walk slowly.

OLD IDEAS

Scientists once thought the stegosaurus walked on two legs!

The dinosaur had a narrow head with a pointed beak. Four spikes stuck out from the end of its tail.

spike

⚠️ SIZE CHART

15 feet (5 meters)

10 feet (3 meters)

5 feet (2 meters)

DIET AND DEFENSES

The stegosaurus was an **herbivore**.
Its beak grabbed at low plants.
Its small teeth struggled to **grind** leaves.

Some scientists believe it stood on its back legs to reach leaves on small trees.

The stegosaurus needed a lot of food! But its teeth did not break down plants very well.

The stegosaurus gulped down rocks.
They helped break plants down in
the dinosaur's stomach.

⚠️ ## A WEAK BITE

The stegosaurus's bite was
not strong. It had weaker jaws
than some types of dogs!

⚠️ ## STEGOSAURUS DIET

ferns

moss

pine needles

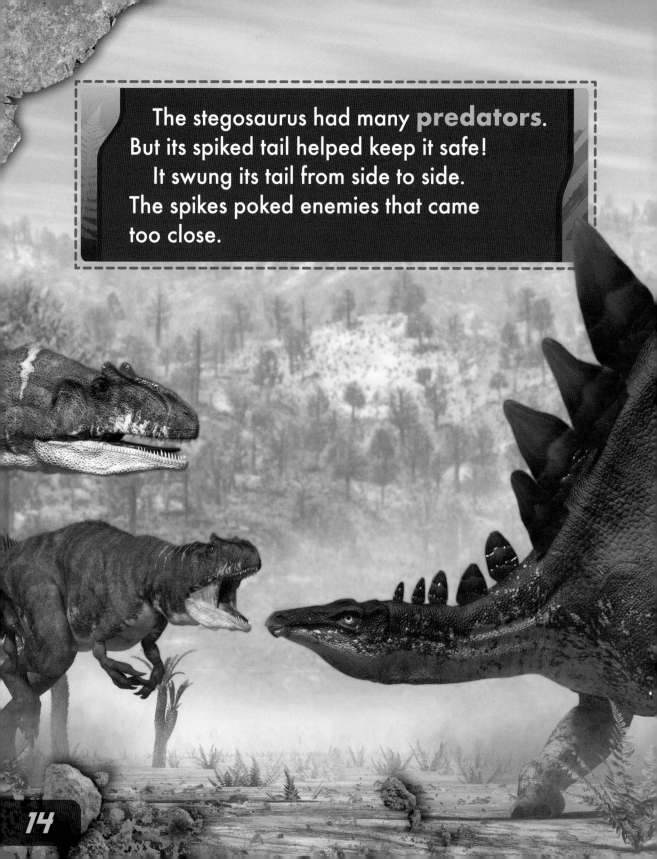

The stegosaurus had many **predators**. But its spiked tail helped keep it safe! It swung its tail from side to side. The spikes poked enemies that came too close.

A HUGE DISCOVERY

The first plate fossil ever found was more than 3 feet (1 meter) long!

FOSSILS AND EXTINCTION

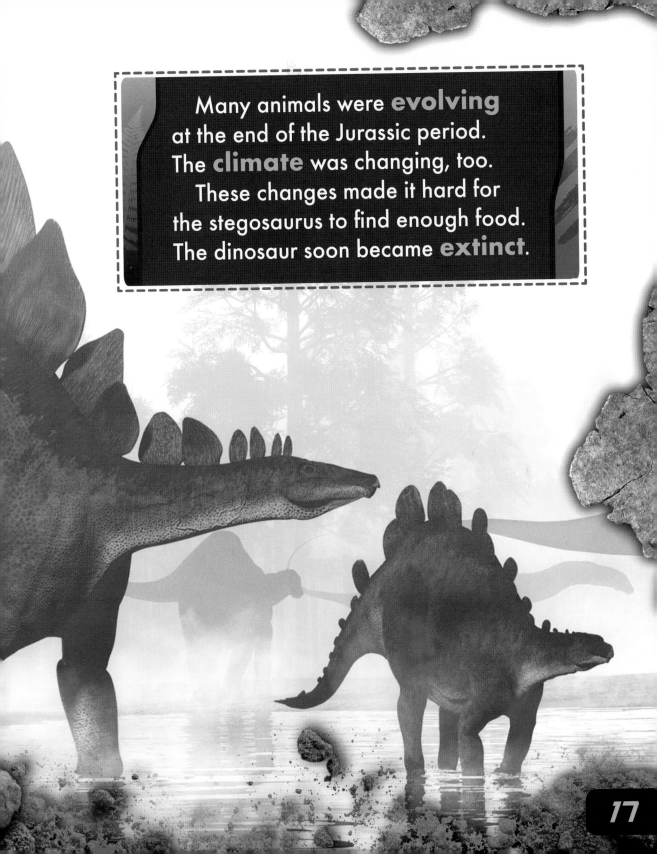

Many animals were **evolving** at the end of the Jurassic period. The **climate** was changing, too. These changes made it hard for the stegosaurus to find enough food. The dinosaur soon became **extinct**.

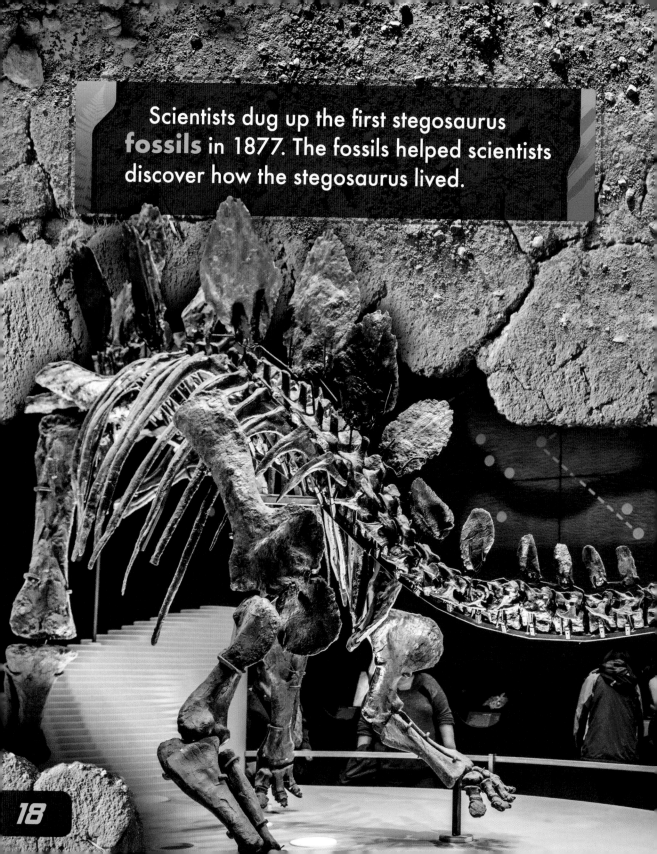

Scientists dug up the first stegosaurus **fossils** in 1877. The fossils helped scientists discover how the stegosaurus lived.

STEGOSAURUS FOSSIL MAP

Canada

United States

Mexico

KEY

○━ fossil site

More studies will help scientists learn even more about the mighty stegosaurus!

GET TO KNOW THE STEGOSAURUS

⚠ FIRST FOSSILS FOUND

1877 in the Morrison Formation near Morrison, Colorado

beak

HEIGHT around 10 feet (3 meters) at the shoulder

⚠ LOCATION

North America

LENGTH up to 30 feet (9 meters) long

plates

⚠️ **FOOD**

ferns   pine needles

tail spikes

⚠️ **FOUND BY**

Arthur Lakes

⚠️ **WEIGHT**   **up to 4,000 pounds (1,814 kilograms)**

GLOSSARY

climate—the usual weather in a certain area over long periods of time

evolving—changing slowly into a better form

extinct—no longer living

fossils—the remains of living things that lived long ago

grind—to break or crush into small pieces

herbivore—an animal that only eats plants

Jurassic period—the second period of the Mesozoic era that occurred between 200 million and 145 million years ago; the Late Jurassic period began around 163 million years ago.

mates—a pair of adult animals that produce babies

predators—animals that hunt other animals for food

TO LEARN MORE

AT THE LIBRARY

Bell, Samantha S. *Stegosaurus*. Lake Elmo, Minn.: Focus Readers, 2018.

Gilbert, Sara. *Stegosaurus*. Mankato, Minn.: Creative Education, 2019.

Waxman, Laura Hamilton. *Discovering Stegosaurus*. Mankato, Minn.: Amicus, 2019.

ON THE WEB

FACTSURFER

Factsurfer.com gives you a safe, fun way to find more information.

1. Go to www.factsurfer.com.

2. Enter "stegosaurus" into the search box and click 🔍.

3. Select your book cover to see a list of related web sites.

INDEX